What I Thought I'd Take To My Grave

Alyssa Heidenreich

India | USA | UK

Presentation by *BookLeaf Publishing*

Web: www.bookleafpub.com

E-mail: info@bookleafpub.com

ISBN: 9789363316423

First edition 2024

My beautiful best friends, Bella and my momma. I couldn't have gotten through this past year without your unwavering belief in me. I am lucky to have experienced unconditional love in this lifetime.

ACKNOWLEDGEMENT

To my greatest loves and most tragic losses:
Thank you for helping me learn and grow.

PREFACE

As someone with OCD and ADHD, there's always a lot of noise in my head. More often than not, it's easier to bury the whirlwind of thoughts and emotions than try to make sense of them. Over the past year or so, I've really aimed to take accountability of my role in managing mental illness. I realized I can no longer compartmentalize trauma, numb feelings, or be ashamed of my flaws and past. Thus, this special collection, my first published poetry book, was born. Thank you for reading.

touch

i said "no" so many times; you should've heard
me.

my sunshine

oh, how lovely it is that he welcomes the stain of
mauve lipstick upon his neck
wraps my thighs in heavy breath and tattoos
them with love bites to veil ancestral scars
an umbrella cloaking me in safety from down
pouring fear
my sunshine blinding melancholy and glittering
the skies

hours

where are you?
said you were on the way at ten
and now it's two a.m.
but i'm afraid to be alone.
that's why i'll still open the door
when you finally care enough to show.

thanks for teaching me how to laugh

a simple situation where we get drunk and high
and fuck
pester each other for fun and avoid uttering
anything serious
long to say, "i love you," but save peace because
we know that this is such a simple situation
and complexity hurts to last
though after once losing my smile, i can thank
you for teaching me how to laugh

woman

she looks like a delicate butterfly
tastes like ripened cherries
smells like salty ocean air
sounds like twinkling chimes
feels like a warm embrace
these senses melt into a hush set at dusk
a quiet tease and delicious view
she is divine feminine

random act of kindness

ready for pick up: a maltese dog-shaped cake.
mom and i venture to the marsh bakery. we chat
up a man in line who's son shares my birthday. i
turn 8 on the 8th, and he turns 18.

i ask the man if his son is getting a maltese
dog-shaped cake, too. he giggles as from behind
the counter, a lady with short silver hair hands
him a cookie cake. i think, what a shame for his
son to not get a birthday cake, considering
cookies aren't actually cake. but i have manners,
so when mr. cookie says his goodbyes, i wave.

just as the lady with short silver hair hands me
the maltese dog-shaped cake, he reappears and
hands me a bouquet of shiny red roses. i find this
creepy... like i'm cute, but way too young for
him, and i'll have to see a picture of him son
first. mr. cookie explains that me and mom's
conversation was a gift to him, so this is his gift
to me. apparently, he never actually gets to see
his son since he's in heaven, so each year, he sets
two plates of cookie cake down at the dinner
table: one at his chair and one at an empty chair.
he sheds a tear, and so does mom. i can't stop

thinking about how brutal it is that even though he's in heaven, the son still doesn't get a maltese-dog shaped cake.

now that we have mine, mom and i turn to leave. the lady with short silver hair wishes me happy birthday one more time, then she barks, pretending to be my maltese-dog shaped cake. this is ridiculous, as she clearly works behind the counter at the marsh bakery. even an 8-year-old can see that.

i've never been good at letting myself grieve

i've never been good at letting myself grieve.
i attempt the role of valiant one piecing
fragments together after tragedy.
press my thoughts into a box too small to encase
them all, so it must bend.
it inevitably breaks with a crash of emotion like
vigorous hurricane currents,
and i rebuild by manifesting more problems
once i begin to feel again.
that's why i've never been good at letting myself
grieve-
always doing too much or too little,
when will i feel like i'm doing it right?

the siren

a siren shrouded in the sea
spots a ship and sings it's sailors to sleep
she sows both sorrow and sapphire graves
a heartbreaker, a man-eater
i am the siren

the space between

hundreds of miles bar us from locking lips and
sharing sweat,
but what are miles but mere inches on a
roadmap?

sixth grade bullies

sixth grade social studies with mr. h.

i sit at a table in front of his desk, working on a
group project without a group. to his right is
another table, where a group of two girls and
one boy aren't working on their project. they're
huddled close together, whispering and laughing.
personally, i never huddle during class; i get my
work done. i draw dots on a yellow map with a
fat marker.

out of nowhere, mr. h., who doesn't interact with
me often unless it's to grade my solo-group
projects, boasts, "alyssa, is that a new sweater?"
my sweater is new, and it is lavender and sparkly
and v-necky and kinda itchy and from the
junior's plus section at jcpenney. i grin.

"yes. i just got it at jcpenney!" he may need to
know that. what if he has a daughter or niece
that shops their junior's plus section?

the group without a project whispers and laughs
and i glance their way, not because i'm trying to
stare, but because they're making too much noise

and very few dots on yellow maps with fat
markers. for a second, i lock eyes with the girl
emily, who was glancing at me first. i notice she
has ice blue eyes that strongly contrast her
strawberry blond hair. they look like husky eyes.
she's really pretty and seems nice.

mr. h slams down his coffee mug and loudly
clears his throat. now, he grins. "it looks very
nice on you. purple is really your color!" i grin
again and draw some more dots. it was so nice
of mr. h to say something about my sweater.

i'm certain i inspired the group without a project
today, too. they're no longer huddled, whispering
and laughing, but they still stare at my lavender,
sparkly, y-necky, kinda itchy, from the junior's
plus size section at jcpenney sweater. especially
emily. she's stares, like, really hard, to the point
she almost doesn't look nice anymore. almost. i
feel bad that she's so jealous of my sweater.

the door

the door sighed shut, signaling our end
but i'd tear it off the hinges just to start with you
again

paragraphs

sending paragraphs i know you won't even read
does it feel better to get all this shit off my chest,
or would there be more power in leaving things
unsaid?

borderline

i'm an expert and pushing and pulling away
just know i only hurt you because i wanted you
to stay

burying an era

each meaningless touch from another man
grinds me into finer sand,
freezes tender violet bruises and cloaks
forbearance in river styx.
their enchantment reveals: curiosity is death,
bliss is opportunity,
and i am a summoner...
fibers akin plucked feathers sleepily drifting
toward the floor,
are the ghosts of your fingerprints that brand this
soul no more.

growing, growing, gone

once planted as a minuscule seed,
sensitivity breaks through ruddy clay
and sprouts into a spiky succulent.
she's beautiful and finally has the spine
to fashion a fortress that blocks forthcoming
ache.

stay in today

tomorrow, i will worry. tonight, i must quiet my mind.

mourn again

they say the body keeps the score
well, we're approaching one year
and the wounds have unstitched
the clock strikes "bleed anew"

an apology

though there's much to apologize for- movie
reels full of deception and greed and lack of
accountability,
i'm mostly sorry for not owning enough respect
to abandon my bleak self-fulfilling prophecy.

am i allowed to?

after a five-day deep sleep, your brain was
released to a hospital bed
the first thing you ate upon waking was refried
beans
i fed them to your swollen black eyes and
scabbed-over face
in a restaurant of a billion tubes and loud
machines

after a decade, i still view dissociation's gothic
portrait
you weren't fully there, and still aren't quite...
funny, now i eat lots of beans while while i
ponder,
how can you grieve someone that's still alive?

peonies

i'm so jaded from permitting such monsters to
fountain tears into the vases that are my eyes,
but at least now they are home to flowers.

the next life

please search for me in twenty years
when you are there and i am here
despite the space between, we're always near
because

we both crashed our cars and went to ERs
spun turntables and drank at hotel bars
shared all our trauma, tears, and biggest fears

crafted evil texts, then had make-up sex
cooked lots of pasta and raised lots of pets
daydreamed a homestead with blue-eyed babies

snoozed on the couch to scary flix
skipped town for fests, planned future road-trips
created love and art on ecstacy

broke both our hearts, gave them to new lovers
still snuck phone calls and linked under covers
numbed our shame and memories with cocaine

in twenty years, my plea won't win
since you'll have her and i'll have him
but we promised to meet again in the next life